ht big small many few asleep awake
ntry old new inside outside part whole
ard soft day night big small many few
fast slow city country old new inside
p down a little alot hard soft day night
sunny empty full fast slow city country
alistic abstract up down a little alot
asleep awake rainy sunny empty full
outside part whole realistic abstract
ht big small many few asleep awake
ntry old new inside outside part whole
ard soft day night big small many few
fast slow city country old new inside
p down a little alot hard soft day night
sunny empty full fast slow city country
alistic abstract up down a little alot
asleep awake rainy sunny empty full
outside part whole rea... stract wake
ht big small many few...

ntry old new inside outside part whole
d soft day night big small many few
st slow city country old new inside
down a little alot hard soft day night

This book is dedicated to Owen, Wade, and Cara Tressider, and Christian and Holden Jackson by their grandmother, Marie-Louise Jackson, who wishes them a lifetime of joyful reading.

Art Museum
Opposites

Katy Friedland
Marla K. Shoemaker

Philadelphia Museum of Art
in association with

TEMPLE
UNIVERSITY PRESS

Philadelphia

A Welcome from the Director

Art museums provide endless opportunities for learning and wonder. In their galleries we experience works of art in two different, but complementary ways—individually and in relation to each other—and learn different, but equally valuable things in the process. Museum educators Katy Friedland and Marla K. Shoemaker explore the theme of comparing in this lovely—and lively—publication, their second children's book featuring objects from the collections of the Philadelphia Museum of Art. They have selected works of art that, when paired, can help us learn about contrasts and about the meanings of opposites such as *day/night*, *many/few*, and *inside/outside*. Along the way, the authors invite children and adults to look more closely at these wonderful objects and marvel at the new possibilities they reveal.

We are delighted that a dear friend of the Museum, Marie-Louise Jackson, has once again generously lent her support to a children's book, this one in honor of her grandchildren, Owen, Wade, Cara, Christian, and Holden. May they and all children be inspired to experience the wonder of art wherever it is encountered, either between the covers of this book or within the walls of a museum!

Timothy Rub
The George D. Widener Director and Chief Executive Officer
Philadelphia Museum of Art

up
the stairs

down the stairs

In each picture find the curving staircase and follow it with your finger. Which painting shows a young man climbing **up the stairs**? Which shows someone going **down the stairs**? What else makes the pictures different from each other?

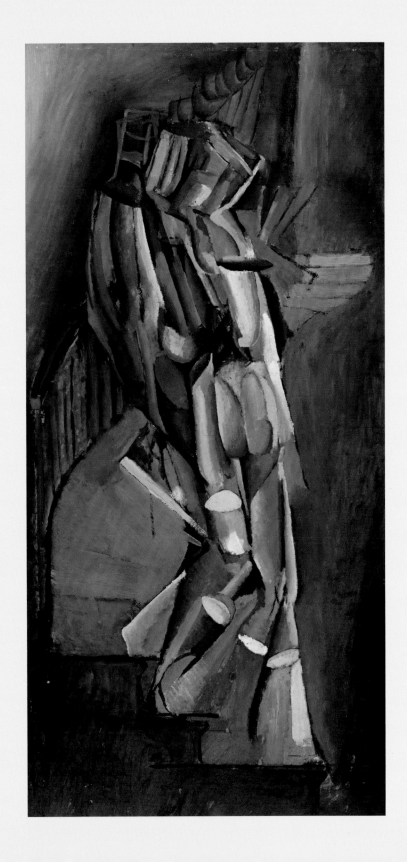

Marcel Duchamp, *Nude Descending a Staircase (No. 1)*, 1911

Facing page: Charles Willson Peale, *Staircase Group (Portrait of Raphaelle Peale and Titian Ramsay Peale)*, 1795

a little

Look at all the red string! One designer used **a little** string to make a seat that looks like a spider's web. The other chair has **a lot** of string. You can barely see its silver frame! Which chair would you like to sit on? Why?

Plan-O-Spider Patio Chair, designed by Hoffer, 1958

Facing page: *Vermelha* (*Red*) Chair, designed by Fernando Campana and Humberto Campana, 1993

a lot

hard

One hat is made of **hard** metal. The other is made of **soft**, tiny feathers. The hard hat is heavy. The soft hat is light. Its feathers can move gently in the wind. Which hat would you like to wear? Where would you go in your hat and what would you do?

Sallet, made in Italy, probably Brescia, c. 1450

soft

Hat, designed by Cristóbal
Balenciaga, 1962

day

Look at the sky in each painting. Do you see a bright red sun? Can you find a small white moon? What colors make up the **day** picture? What colors create a feeling of **night**? These pictures are mysterious! Pick one and make up a story about what is happening.

Marc Chagall, *A Wheatfield on a Summer's Afternoon*, 1942

night

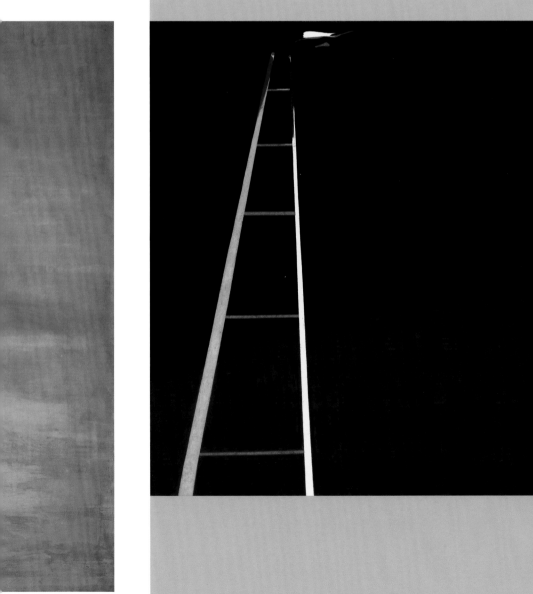

Joan Miró, *Dog Barking at the Moon*, 1926

big

Nandi, the Sacred Bull of Shiva; made in India, Karnataka, Mysore region, c. 1200–1250

small

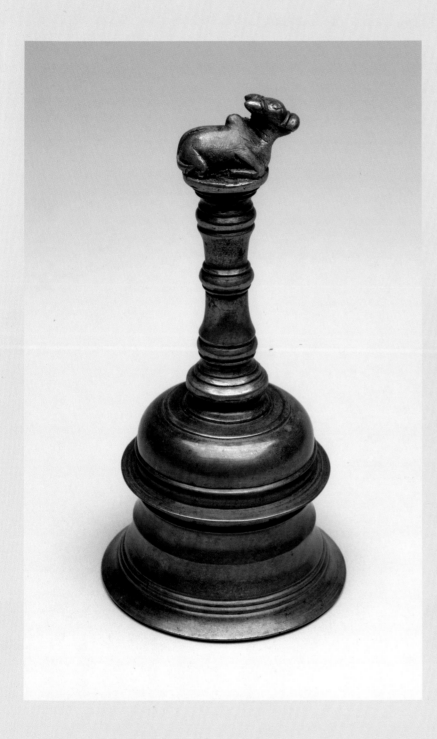

Bulls are very **big**! The stone sculpture is also big. It shows the bull Nandi, resting quietly and decorated with flowers and jewelry. Can you find another sculpture of Nandi? It is very, very **small**—so small it fits on top of a bell's handle! Is this Nandi decorated, too?

Bell with Nandi, the Sacred Bull of Shiva; made in India, nineteenth–mid-twentieth century

many

Jim Hodges, *Every Touch*, 1995
Facing page: Georgia O'Keeffe, *Two Calla Lilies on Pink*, 1928

few

One artist sewed together silk flowers to make a delicate curtain. There are so **many** flowers it is hard to count them all! What colors do you see? The other artist painted just a **few** flowers. She liked painting nature up close. You can see down into each flower's center!

asleep

Look at the children cuddling in grown-ups' arms. In one picture everyone is fast **asleep**. In the other people are wide **awake**. Which picture is colorful? Which one shows lots of fingers and toes? How else are the pictures different?

José Diego María Rivera, *Sleep*, 1932

awake

Mary Stevenson Cassatt, *Mother and Child*, 1908

rainy

Vincent Willem van Gogh, *Rain*, 1889

sunny

One artist painted a wet, **rainy** day. Can you see the raindrops? Find a wall around a field. The **sunny** picture has a wall, too! Do you see its shadow? Look hard for a woman holding a black umbrella—not to keep out rain, but to shade from the sun!

Giovanni Boldini, *Highway of Combes-la-Ville*, 1873

empty

The trash can is **empty**—completely empty! You can see right through to the bottom. The pot is **full** of mussels—so full its lid can't close! Mussels are shellfish that are yummy to eat. Imagine lifting these containers. Which one would feel light? Which would feel heavy?

Garbino Can, designed by Karim Rashid, 1996

full

Marcel Broodthaers, *The Triumph of Mussels*, 1965

fast

 Olympische Spiele München 1972

slow

Five men are running **fast**! They are wearing colorful clothes and spiked shoes. Which runner will win the race? In the other picture a little girl is taking **slow** steps up a hill. She is carrying a heavy basket of laundry and an umbrella. Something else is walking slowly. What is it?

Pierre Bonnard, *Little Laundry Girl*, c. 1895–96
Facing page: Jacob Lawrence, *Olympic Games Munich 1972*, 1971–72

city

In the **city**, buildings are crowded together. Find a chimney, railings, and windows. Do you see the boat? In the **country**, there are large, open spaces and few buildings. Can you find cows, flowers, and trees? What sound do cows make?

Fernand Léger, *Animated Landscape*, 1924

country

Winslow Homer, *A Temperance Meeting*, 1874

old

The **old** chair has lots of carved designs. More than one hundred years later, an artist designed a **new** chair that reminds us of the old one. Can you find shapes and patterns that are the same on both chairs? How are the chairs different? Which is your favorite?

Side Chair, made in New York, 1845–60

new

Gothic Revival Chair, designed by Robert Venturi, 1984

inside

A monkey is **inside** an artist's studio! What else is in the room? **Outside**, monkeys are playing in a lush, green jungle. Look at all the different leaf shapes! The monkey inside is playing a horn. What sounds will the monkeys outside make?

Antoine Vollon, *Monkey in a Studio*, 1869
Facing page: Henri-Julien-Félix Rousseau, *The Merry Jesters*, 1906

outside

part

The photograph shows **part** of a cat. Find its eyes, nose, and whiskers. The sculpture shows a **whole** cat. Do you see its ears, paws, and tail? Long ago this cat was used as a nightlight. A candle's flickering light would shine through its

whole

Lantern in the Form of a Tortoiseshell Cat, made in China, Qing dynasty, Kangxi period (1662–1722)
Facing page: André Kertész, *Siamese Cat*, *Paris*, 1928

realistic

One painting is **realistic**. It shows every detail. Can you find eggs in a bird's nest? The other picture is **abstract**. The artist painted the feeling and memory of blue flowers in gardens near her home. Can you draw an abstract picture of something you remember?

Severin Roesen, *Flower Still Life with Bird's Nest*, 1853
Facing page: Alma Thomas, *Hydrangeas Spring Song*, 1976

abstract

A Note to Grown-Ups

Even at a very young age, children employ the basic perceptual skills of comparing and contrasting in order to understand the world around them. By pairing opposite words with works of art, this book encourages children to think about the differences between words such as *day* and *night*, as well as between the objects presented on each spread. But there are many other fun and educational ways to explore the art on these pages! Here are a few ideas:

Flip through the book and look for similarities instead of opposites. How many chairs can you find? How many times do you see the color red?

Become a family of artists! Take out your drawing materials and pick your favorite work of art in the book. Can you create your own opposite picture? Try using different lines or contrasting colors.

Use your imagination! Make up a story about one of the objects. How would you use the object? What is happening in the picture? Pretend the people or animals in the pictures could talk. What would they say to you? What would you say to them?

Finally, if you are in Philadelphia, visit the Philadelphia Museum of Art to see some of these works firsthand. (The Museum is constantly changing, so they might not all be on view at the same time.) If you are not in Philadelphia, go to your local art museum and play some of these games. Find objects that illustrate other opposites such as *young/old* or *light/dark*. Looking at art together will reveal things you would never see by yourself!

Illustrations

up the stairs
Charles Willson Peale
American, 1741–1827
Staircase Group (Portrait of Raphaelle Peale and Titian Ramsay Peale)
1795
Oil on canvas
7 feet 5 1/2 inches x 3 feet 3 3/8 inches (2.3 x 1 m)
The George W. Elkins Collection, E1945-1-1

down the stairs
Marcel Duchamp
American, born France, 1887–1968
Nude Descending a Staircase (No. 1)
1911
Oil on cardboard on panel
37 3/4 x 23 3/4 inches (95.9 x 60.3 cm)
The Louise and Walter Arensberg Collection, 1950-134-58

a little
Plan-O-Spider Patio Chair
Designed by Hoffer (France)
Made by Plan (France)
Designed 1958
Enameled metal and bungee cord
28 x 30 x 30 inches (71.1 x 76.2 x 76.2 cm)
Gift of Jeanne S. Rymer, 2007-186-10

a lot
Vermelha (Red) Chair
Designed by Fernando Campana (Brazilian, born 1961) and Humberto Campana (Brazilian, born 1953)
Made by Edra S.p.A. (Perignano, Italy, active 1987–present)
Designed 1993
Epoxy powder-coated steel, aluminum, cotton-covered acrylic cord, and metalized polyester mixed with polyamide
30 1/4 x 34 x 28 inches (76.8 x 86.4 x 71.1 cm)
Gift of Edra S.p.A., Perignano, Italy, 2004-6-1

hard
Sallet
Made in Italy, probably Brescia
c. 1450
Steel
11 x 8 1/4 x 9 15/16 inches (28 x 21 x 25.2 cm)
Bequest of Carl Otto Kretzschmar von Kienbusch, 1977-167-55

soft
Hat
Designed by Cristóbal Balenciaga (Spanish, active Spain and France; 1895–1972)
1962
Ostrich feathers with silk satin bow
Gift of Mr. and Mrs. Rodolphe Meyer de Schauensee, 1978-156-26

day
Marc Chagall
French, born Belorussia, 1887–1985
A Wheatfield on a Summer's Afternoon
1942
Tempera on fabric
30 x 50 feet (9.1 x 15.2 m)
Gift of Leslie and Stanley Westreich, 1986-173-1

night
Joan Miró
Spanish, 1893–1983
Dog Barking at the Moon
1926
Oil on canvas
28 3/4 x 36 1/4 inches (73 x 92.1 cm)
A. E. Gallatin Collection, 1952-61-82

big
Nandi, the Sacred Bull of Shiva
Made in India, Karnataka, Mysore region
Hoyshala dynasty
c. 1200–1250
Schist
Length 31 3/4 inches (80.6 cm)
Purchased with the Joseph E. Temple Fund, 1966-123-1

small
Bell with Nandi, the Sacred Bull of Shiva
Made in India
Nineteenth–mid-twentieth century
Copper alloy
Height 7 inches (17.8 cm); diameter 3 3/8 inches (8.6 cm)
Stella Kramrisch Collection, 1994-148-282

many
Jim Hodges
American, born 1957
Every Touch
1995
Silk
14 x 16 feet (4.3 x 4.9 m)
Purchased with funds contributed by Mr. and Mrs. W. B. Dixon Stroud, 1995-55-1

few
Georgia O'Keeffe
American, 1887–1986
Two Calla Lilies on Pink
1928
Oil on canvas
40 x 30 inches (101.6 x 76.2 cm)
Bequest of Georgia O'Keeffe for the Alfred Stieglitz Collection, 1987-70-4

asleep
José Diego María Rivera
Mexican, 1886–1957
Sleep (Sueño)
1932
Lithograph
Image 16 15/16 x 11 7/8 inches (43 x 30.2 cm)
Sheet 22 5/8 x 15 15/16 inches (57.5 x 40.5 cm)
Printed by George C. Miller, New York
Published by Weyhe Gallery, New York
Gift of R. Sturgis and Marion B. F. Ingersoll, 1943-35-24

awake
Mary Stevenson Cassatt
American, 1844–1926
Mother and Child
1908
Oil on canvas
32 x 23 7/8 inches (81.3 x 60.6 cm)
The Alex Simpson, Jr., Collection, 1928-63-3

rainy
Vincent Willem van Gogh
Dutch, 1853–1890
Rain
1889
Oil on canvas
28 7/8 x 36 3/8 inches (73.3 x 92.4 cm)
The Henry P. McIlhenny Collection in memory of Frances P. McIlhenny, 1986-26-36

sunny
Giovanni Boldini
Italian, 1842–1931
Highway of Combes-la-Ville
1873
Oil on canvas
27 1/4 x 39 15/16 inches (69.2 x 101.4 cm)
The George W. Elkins Collection, E1924-4-2

empty
Garbino Can
Designed by Karim Rashid (Canadian, born Egypt, born 1960)
Made by Umbra, Ltd. (Toronto, active 1979–present)
Designed 1996
Molded polypropylene
13 x 10 x 10 1/2 inches (33 x 25.4 x 26.7 cm)
Gift of Umbra, Ltd., 1999-107-4

full
Marcel Broodthaers
Belgian, 1924–1976
The Triumph of Mussels (Triomphe de Moules I [Moules Casserole])
1965
Painted and enameled iron alloy, and mussel shells with paint
18 1/2 x 19 5/8 x 14 5/8 inches (47 x 49.8 x 37.1 cm)
Gift (by exchange) of Mr. and Mrs. R. Sturgis Ingersoll and Mrs. Herbert Cameron Morris, 1997-43-1

fast

Jacob Lawrence
American, 1917–2000
Olympic Games Munich 1972 (Olympische Spiele München 1972)
1971–72
Color screenprint
Image 34 3/8 x 25 3/16 inches (87.3 x 64 cm)
Sheet 40 x 25 3/16 inches (101.6 x 64 cm)
Gift of Marla K. Shoemaker, 2002-60-1

slow

Pierre Bonnard
French, 1867–1947
Little Laundry Girl
From *L'Album des peintres-graveurs* (Paris: Ambroise Vollard, 1896)
c. 1895–96
Color lithograph
Edition 40/100
Image 11 9/16 x 7 3/4 inches (29.4 x 19.7 cm)
Purchased with the John D. McIlhenny Fund, 1941-8-14

city

Fernand Léger
French, 1881–1955
Animated Landscape
1924
Oil on canvas
19 1/2 x 25 5/8 inches (49.5 x 65.1 cm)
Gift of Bernard Davis, 1950-63-1

country

Winslow Homer
American, 1836–1910
A Temperance Meeting
1874
Oil on canvas
20 3/8 x 30 1/8 inches (51.8 x 76.5 cm)
Purchased with the John Howard McFadden, Jr., Fund, 1956-118-1

old

Side Chair
Made in New York
1845–60
Walnut
47 3/4 x 18 3/8 x 25 inches (121.3 x 46.7 x 63.5 cm)
Gift of Joan Prentice von Erdberg, 1979-112-3

new

***Gothic Revival* Chair**
Designed by Robert Venturi (American, born 1925)
Made by Knoll (East Greenville, Pennsylvania, active 1938–present)
Designed 1979–84; made 1984
Bent laminated wood and painted plastic laminate
40 3/4 x 20 1/4 x 23 inches (103.5 x 51.4 x 58.4 cm)
Gift of Marion Boulton Stroud, 1999-158-1

inside

Antoine Vollon
French, 1833–1900
Monkey in a Studio
1869
Oil on panel
18 1/8 x 14 5/8 inches (46 x 37.1 cm)
John G. Johnson Collection, 1917. Cat. 1108

outside

Henri-Julien-Félix Rousseau
French, 1844–1910
The Merry Jesters
1906
Oil on canvas
57 3/8 x 44 5/8 inches (145.7 x 113.3 cm)
The Louise and Walter Arensberg Collection, 1950-134-176

part

André Kertész
American, born Hungary, 1894–1985
Siamese Cat, Paris
1928
Gelatin silver print
Image and sheet 6 5/16 x 6 7/8 inches (16 x 17.5 cm)
The Lynne and Harold Honickman Gift of the Julien Levy Collection, 2001-62-596

whole

Lantern in the Form of a Tortoiseshell Cat
Made in China
Qing dynasty (1644–1911), Kangxi period (1662–1722)
Porcelain with overglaze enamel decoration
3 7/8 x 6 inches (9.8 x 15.2 cm)
The Alfred and Margaret Caspary Memorial Gift, 1955-50-346

realistic

Severin Roesen
American, born Germany, 1815/16–c. 1872
Flower Still Life with Bird's Nest
1853
Oil on canvas
40 x 32 inches (101.6 x 81.3 cm)
Purchased with support from The Henry P. McIlhenny Fund in memory of Frances P. McIlhenny; Mr. and Mrs. Robert L. McNeil, Jr.; The Edith H. Bell Fund; Mrs. J. Maxwell Moran; Marguerite and Gerry Lenfest; The Center for American Art Acquisition Fund; Donna C. and Morris W. Stroud II; Dr. and Mrs. Robert E. Booth, Jr.; Frederick LaValley and John Whitenight; Mr. and Mrs. John A. Nyheim; Charlene Sussel; Penelope P. Wilson; and the American Art Committee, 2010-6-1

abstract

Alma Thomas
American, 1891–1978
Hydrangeas Spring Song
1976
Acrylic on canvas
6 feet 6 inches x 4 feet (2 x 1.2 m)
Purchased with funds contributed by Mr. and Mrs. Julius Rosenwald II in honor of René and Sarah Carr d'Harnoncourt, The Judith Rothschild Foundation, and with other funds being raised in honor of the 125th Anniversary of the Museum and in celebration of African American art, 2002-20-1

Acknowledgments

The authors wish to thank the following people for their invaluable assistance in making this book a reality: Cristin O'Keefe Aptowicz; Sherry Babbitt; Peter Barberie; David L. Barquist; Carlos Basualdo; Richard Bonk; Tony L. Brown, Sophie Sanders, and Samuel Solomon Sanders; Conna Clark; Megan and Jonas Cohen; Donna Corbin; Judy Dion; Felice Fischer; Kathleen A. Foster; Holly Frisbee; Stuart D. Gerstein; Jennifer Ginsberg; H. Kristina Haugland; Andrea Hemmann; Kathryn Bloom Hiesinger; John W. Ittmann; Alexandra Alevizatos Kirtley; Shelley R. Langdale; Darielle Mason; Mark Mitchell; Sarah Noreika; Joseph J. Rishel; Timothy Rub; Shannon Schuler; Mimi B. Stein; Michael Taylor; Pierre Terjanian; Jennifer Thompson; Leslie Essoglou Vasilyev; Jason Wierzbicki; Bethany Wiggin and Teddy Helgerson; and Graydon Wood. Finally, they thank Greg and Jason for tirelessly looking over the pages of this book.

Photography Credits

Aomori Museum of Art, Japan: *day*; Dave DiRentis: frontispiece; Mark Garvin: p. 36; Jason Hickey: *inside*; Eric Mitchell: *awake*; Andrea Nuñez: *empty*; Lynn Rosenthal: *big*, *many*, *slow*; Jason Wierzbicki: *asleep*, *country*, *part*; Graydon Wood: p. 4, *up the stairs*, *down the stairs*, *small*, *a little*, *a lot*, *night*, *hard*, *soft*, *few*, *rainy*, *sunny*, *full*, *fast*, *city*, *old*, *new*, *outside*, *whole*, *abstract*, back cover (left and right)

Front cover: Marc Chagall, *A Wheatfield on a Summer's Afternoon*, detail, 1942 (left); Joan Miró, *Dog Barking at the Moon*, detail, 1926 (right)

Back cover: East Entrance of the Philadelphia Museum of Art during the day (left) and at night (right)

Frontispiece: Julien Friedland dancing to the music of Penn Sargam in the Indian Temple Hall at the Philadelphia Museum of Art

Page 4 (left to right): Sophie Sanders, Tony L. Brown, and Samuel Solomon Sanders looking at *Portrait of Anthony Reyniers and His Family* by Cornelis de Vos (Flemish, active Antwerp; 1584/85–1651). Detail; 1631, oil on canvas, 5 feet 7 inches x 8 feet ½ inch (1.7 x 2.5 m). Philadelphia Museum of Art. Purchased with the W. P. Wilstach Fund, W1902-1-22

Page 36: Visitors participating in Early Bird Read and Look, a program that invites preschoolers and their families to enjoy picture books and art projects in the Philadelphia Museum of Art's galleries

Library of Congress Cataloging-in-Publication Data

Friedland, Katy, 1978–
  Art museum opposites / Katy Friedland, Marla K. Shoemaker.
    p. cm.
  ISBN 978-0-87633-222-1 (pma hardcover)—
  ISBN 978-1-4399-0523-4 (tup hardcover)
  1. Art—Juvenile literature. 2. Polarity—Juvenile literature. I. Shoemaker, Marla K., 1951– II. Title.
  N5308.F755 2010
  700—dc22
              2010020731

Produced by the Publishing Department
Philadelphia Museum of Art
Sherry Babbitt, The William T. Ranney Director of Publishing
2525 Pennsylvania Avenue
Philadelphia, PA 19130
www.philamuseum.org

Published in association with Temple University Press
Philadelphia, PA 19122
www.temple.edu/tempress

Edited by Sarah Noreika
Production by Richard Bonk
Designed by Andrea Hemmann, GHI Design, Philadelphia
Printed and bound in Singapore by Tien Wah Press Pte Ltd
20 19 18 17 16 15 14 13 12 11 10   1 2 3 4 5 6 7 8 9